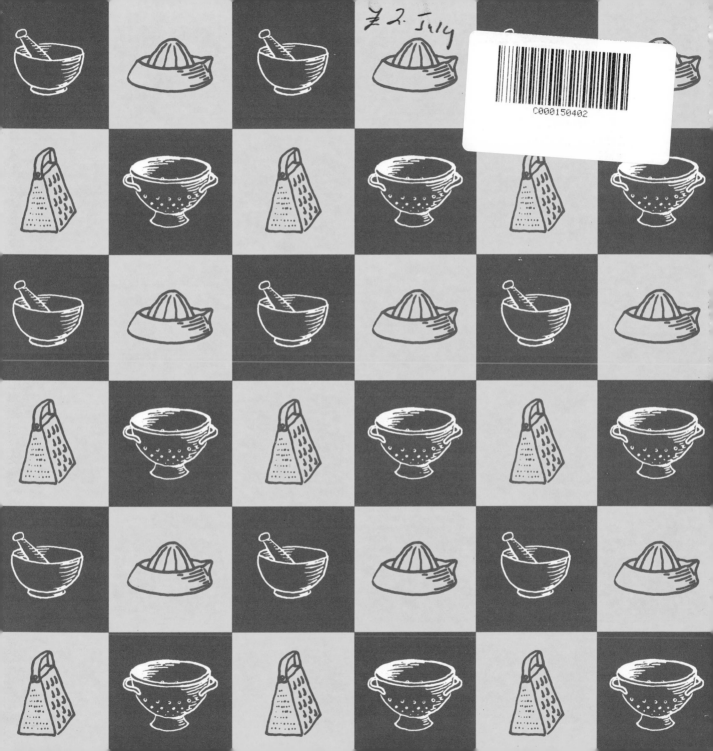

PARSLEY

PARSLEY

A Book of Recipes

INTRODUCTION BY CHRIS INGRAM

LORENZ BOOKS

First published in 1998 by Lorenz Books

© Anness Publishing Limited 1998

Lorenz Books is an imprint of
Anness Publishing Limited
Hermes House
88–89 Blackfriars Road
London SE1 8HA

ISBN 1 85967 552 2

A CIP catalogue record for this book is available from the British Library

Publisher Joanna Lorenz
Senior Cookery Editor Linda Fraser
Project Editor Margaret Malone
Designer Bill Mason
Illustrations Anna Koska

Photographers Karl Adamson, William Adams-Lingwood, Edward Allwright, Steve Baxter, James Duncan,
John Freeman, Michelle Garrett, Amanda Heywood, Don Last and Patrick McLeavey
Recipes Carla Capalbo, Maxine Clark, Andi Clevely, Christine France, Silvana Franco, Shirley Gill, Christine Ingram, Sue Maggs,
Annie Nichols, Katherine Richmond, Liz Trigg, Hilaire Walden, Laura Washburn and Steven Wheeler
Stylists Madeleine Brehaut, Hilary Guy, Blake Minton, Fiona Tillett and Elizabeth Wolf-Cohen
Jacket photography Janine Hosegood

For all recipes, quantities are given in both metric and imperial measures and, where appropriate,
measures are also given in standard cups and spoons. Follow one set, but not a mixture,
because they are not interchangeable.

Printed and bound in China

1 3 5 7 9 10 8 6 4 2

Contents

$\mathcal{I}$NTRODUCTION

Parsley has a very special place in the kitchen. Its mild unassuming flavour makes it the most versatile of herbs, adding a fine delicate flavour to an almost limitless number of savoury dishes. Many herbs make their presence known in quite forceful ways. Cuisines, like Italian, Turkish and Thai, can be defined by their well-flavoured aromatic or pungent herbs. Yet in all these cuisines, parsley is never forgotten. It may play a quieter, more modest role than its racier cousins, but it is still among the most widely used of herbs, appreciated for its subtle aromatic flavour and its vibrant colour.

Parsley is native to southern Europe and was grown by the ancient Greeks, who used the herb for ceremonial and medicinal purposes as well as in salads and sauces. During the Isthmian games, victors would be crowned with wreaths of parsley and it was also laid upon the tombs of the dead. The Romans appreciated parsley as a food and introduced it to Britain where it flourished in the moderate climate.

Enthusiasm for parsley continued throughout the centuries. Since it could be grown so successfully in England it remained popular, unlike many of the herbs introduced from southern Europe. During the Middle Ages, people would have grown the herb both for culinary and medicinal uses, as it was considered useful for a number of ailments. This reputation has found its way into stories too. Beatrix Potter's Peter Rabbit, after gorging himself on Mr McGregor's vegetable garden, finally nibbles on parsley to settle his stomach!

Indeed, parsley is one of the most nutritious of herbs. It is particularly high in carotene and vitamin C and contains useful amounts of potassium and calcium.

There are three main varieties of parsley. Curly parsley grows most successfully in northern climates and is the most popular in Britain. Flat-leaf or Italian parsley is a less hardy plant than curly parsley and grows best in the warmer climates of southern Europe and the Middle East, where it is used in huge quantities. Turnip-rooted or Hamburg parsley, although a member of the same family, is not used as a herb, but its roots are eaten as a vegetable.

The wonderful selection of recipes in this book, which concentrate on curly and flat leaf parsley, is a sound testimony to the versatility of this extraordinary herb. From soups and stocks to classic sauces and stuffings, this book serves as the perfect guide to the many culinary uses of this gentle herb.

Types of Parsley

Curly parsley

Sometimes called English parsley, this is the most common parsley and is certainly the most easily recognized. It has dark emerald green leaves that vary between very curled and softly curled. It has a good, fresh flavour and is particularly popular as a garnish.

Flat leaf parsley

Also known as Italian parsley, this is the more favoured parsley in European countries, particularly France, Spain and Italy. It has pretty, rather lacy leaves, varying in colour from pale to dark green. It has a more pronounced flavour that is pleasantly aromatic, giving salads and cooked dishes a distinct yet fresh flavour. It also makes a pretty garnish.

Turnip-rooted parsley

This plant is grown mainly for its tapering root which looks rather like a thin parsnip and tastes like a cross between celeriac and parsley. It is also sometimes referred to as Hamburg parsley and, as the name suggests, the plant is popular in Germany where it is used as a root vegetable.

Dried parsley

Dried parsley is widely available, or you can dry your own very easily. Commercially dried parsley has a reputation for having little or no flavour, although it is just about acceptable if there is no alternative and it is used shortly after opening. Store dried parsley in a cool dry place. Once opened, use within 2–3 months. After that, dried parsley tastes much like dust.

Frozen parsley

Flat leaf and curly parsley are available frozen, or you can freeze your own parsley. Commercially frozen parsley comes in conveniently small containers and should be returned to the freezer once you have used what you need. Do not allow it to defrost and then re-freeze, as this could introduce bacteria as well as destroying flavour.

Chopped parsley

Parsley is chopped both in cooking and for garnishing. It can be finely or coarsely chopped, either with a sharp knife or using a herb mill.

Flat leaf

Dried

Fresh chopped

Curly

Frozen chopped

$\mathscr{B}$ASIC $\mathscr{T}$ECHNIQUES

COOKING WITH PARSLEY

CHOPPING PARSLEY
To chop by hand, snip the leaves from the stalks and chop coarsely, bunching the leaves up against a knife. You can also use a herb mill or a coffee mill for small quantities of parsley, and a food processor for larger quantities.

FREEZING PARSLEY
Wash fresh parsley sprigs and shake dry carefully. Place in freezer bags, label and freeze. For chopped parsley, place a tablespoon in ice cube trays and top up with water. The frozen cubes can be added directly to cooked dishes.

MAKING A BOUQUET GARNI
Take three parsley stalks, one small sprig of thyme and one or two bay leaves and tie firmly with string. For a more aromatic bouquet garni, add a twist of orange or lemon peel, a piece of celery and a sprig of marjoram.

DRYING PARSLEY

Use parsley that is absolutely fresh. Tie into bundles and hang from a rack in a warm, dry room, not exceeding 30°C/86°F. Leave for a week, until the leaves are crisp and dry. To keep the parsley dust-free, place brown paper bags over the tops of the bunches, leaving the bottom open to allow air to circulate. Once completely dry, strip the leaves from the stem and place in a jar. Close tightly and check the next day for condensation, which indicates that the leaves are not completely dry. If this is the case, place the parsley on a rack lined with muslin and leave in a warm room for a further 24 hours. Store dried parsley in airtight dark glass or pottery jars.

GROWING YOUR OWN PARSLEY

Parsley will grow happily in a warm place outside the kitchen door, or on the windowsill. It needs plenty of sun, and on warm days should be kept watered or the plant will wither and die. To grow your own parsley, soak the seeds overnight and then sow directly into pots or into the earth in early spring. The soil must be watered regularly with a fine spray during germination. Once the seedlings are big enough to handle, they should be thinned until the plants are about 20cm/8in apart. Parsley seeds are notoriously slow to germinate and a quicker, albeit less satisfying, course would be to buy small plants from your local nursery. These can be kept indoors or outside, in earthenware pots, hanging baskets or in a pretty windowsill arrangement.

PARSLEY, SAGE AND THYME OIL

This pleasantly herby oil is perfect for green salads and stir-fries.

Pour 600ml/1 pint/2½ cups sunflower oil into a sterilized jar and add 50g/2oz/½ cup chopped fresh parsley, 25g/1oz/⅛ cup chopped fresh sage and 50g/2oz/¼ cup chopped fresh thyme. Cover and allow to stand at room temperature for 1 week. Stir or shake occasionally during that time. Strain the oil through a sieve lined with muslin into a sterilized jug and then decant into sterilized bottles, discarding the used herbs. Add a fresh sprig of parsley or thyme for decoration, if liked. Seal the jar carefully, label and store in a cool place. Use within 6 months. Makes 600ml/1 pint/2½ cups.

HOW TO MAKE PARSLEY SAUCE

Parsley sauce is a classic recipe that you will find yourself using for all sorts of dishes. It's essential with white fish, root vegetables and many green vegetables. It's wonderful with broad beans and is the classic accompaniment to ham and gammon. Curly parsley is the more commonly used variety for this traditional English sauce, but flat leaf parsley is excellent, giving a more distinct, aromatic flavour.

Melt 40g/1½oz/3 tbsp butter in a saucepan. Add 20g/¾oz/2 tbsp plain flour and cook gently for 1 minute, stirring all the time.

Gradually stir in 425ml/¾ pint/ 1¾ cups milk, beating until smooth after each addition, to make a smooth sauce. Cook very gently for about 1 minute.

Stir in 45ml/3 tbsp finely chopped fresh parsley and season to taste. For a richer parsley sauce, add 15ml/ 1 tbsp single cream.

PARSLEY KNOW-HOW

• *Most of the flavour of parsley is in the stalks: use these for stocks and bouquets garnis.*

• *The more densely curled the parsley, the better it is for cooking. Flat leaf parsley is always chopped before being added to dishes.*

• *In sauces, add parsley at the last minute so that it simply heats through. As a general rule, parsley should only be heated, not cooked.*

• *An exception to the above is to deep-fry sprigs of parsley and serve them as a fantastic starter or garnish.*

• *Parsley is an essential ingredient in French* fines herbes. *Chop finely with chervil, chives and tarragon and use for omelettes, in stuffings and as a garnish for mushrooms.*

SIMPLE PARSLEY IDEAS

Green sauce: This is a popular Mediterranean sauce that tastes particularly good with fish. Place 40g/1¹/₂oz fresh flat-leaf parsley, 1 garlic clove and 2 shallots in a food processor. Soak a slice of day-old bread in water, squeeze dry and add to the bowl with 10ml/2 tsp rinsed capers and 30ml/2 tbsp white wine vinegar. Add 75ml/5 tbsp olive oil, season and process until well combined but not completely smooth. Pour into a bowl, cover and leave to infuse for 1 hour before serving.

Gremolata: This Italian flavouring is made from very finely chopped lemon or orange rind, garlic and parsley. It is traditionally sprinkled over Osso Buco, but can be used as a garnish for any rich, braised meat dishes.

Parsley butter: Mash 115g/4oz softened unsalted butter and blend with ¹/₂ crushed garlic clove, 15ml/1 tbsp lemon juice and 45ml/3 tbsp chopped fresh parsley. Shape into a log and roll up in greaseproof paper. Chill and slice as required. Alternatively, chill slightly and roll out between sheets of greaseproof paper. Cut into shapes and chill until ready to serve.

Parsley dressing: Place 60ml/4 tbsp olive oil, 30ml/2 tbsp sunflower oil, 15ml/1 tbsp lemon juice and 45ml/3 tbsp chopped fresh parsley in a screw-top jar. Add a pinch of sugar and seasoning, replace the lid and shake well.

Parsley mayonnaise: Stir 40g/1¹/₂oz chopped flat leaf parsley into 225ml/8fl oz/1 cup home-made or bought mayonnaise.

Parsley stuffing: For a stuffing for lamb, turkey or chicken: fry 2–3 snipped streaky bacon rashers with 1 finely chopped onion in a little butter and/or oil. Mix with 75–115g/3–4oz fresh breadcrumbs and 1 diced apple. Add 45ml/3 tbsp chopped fresh parsley and season well. Moisten with lemon juice and a little chicken stock if necessary.

Persillade: Very finely chop 40g/1¹/₂oz fresh flat leaf parsley and mix with 2 very finely chopped shallots or 2 very finely chopped garlic cloves. Add a good pinch of salt and mix well. Stir into casseroles and fish and poultry dishes just before serving for a fresh Provençale flavour.

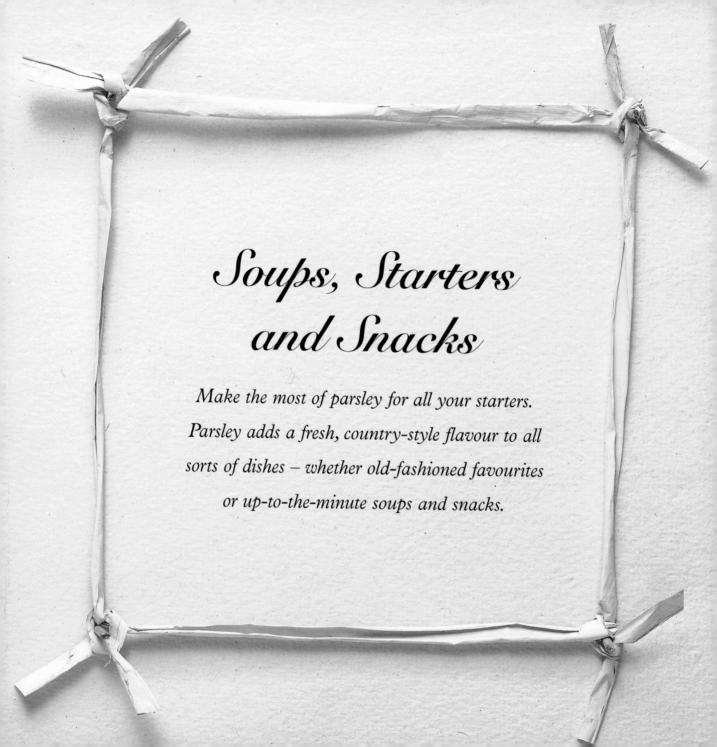

Soups, Starters and Snacks

Make the most of parsley for all your starters.
Parsley adds a fresh, country-style flavour to all
sorts of dishes – whether old-fashioned favourites
or up-to-the-minute soups and snacks.

ITALIAN BEAN AND PARSLEY SOUP

Italian flat leaf parsley adds a fresh, aromatic flavour to this well-flavoured and hearty soup.

Serves 6

*175g/6oz/1 cup dried haricot beans,
  soaked overnight*

*1.75 litres/3 pints/7½ cups chicken
  stock or water*

115g/4oz/1 cup pasta shells

*60ml/4 tbsp olive oil, plus extra,
  to serve*

2 garlic cloves, crushed

*60ml/4 tbsp chopped fresh flat leaf
  parsley*

salt and freshly ground black pepper

COOK'S TIP

*Use medium-size pasta shells or
shapes for this recipe. If using
fresh pasta, simmer for just 5–6
minutes until the pasta is tender.*

Drain the beans and place in a large saucepan with the stock or water. Bring to the boil, boil rapidly for 10 minutes, then lower the heat and simmer, half-covered for 2–2½ hours until the beans are tender. Spoon half of the beans and a little of their cooking liquid into a blender or food processor and blend until smooth. Stir back into the remaining beans in the pan.

Add the pasta and simmer gently for 15 minutes until the pasta is tender, adding a little extra water or stock if the soup seems too thick.

Heat the oil in a small pan and fry the garlic until golden. Stir into the soup with the parsley and season well with salt and pepper. Ladle into warmed soup bowls and drizzle each with a little extra olive oil.

CHICK-PEA AND PARSLEY SOUP

This tasty soup, served with a tangy lemon garnish, comes from Morocco, where parsley is a favourite ingredient. If possible, use flat leaf parsley.

Serves 6

225g/8oz/1¼ cups chick-peas,
  soaked overnight
1 small onion
40g/1½oz fresh flat leaf parsley
30ml/2 tbsp olive and sunflower oil,
  mixed
1.2 litres/2 pints/5 cups chicken stock
juice of ½ lemon
salt and freshly ground black pepper
lemon wedges and finely pared strips
  of rind, to garnish
crusty bread, to serve

COOK'S TIP
*Chick-peas blend better in soups
and other dishes if you rub
away the outer skin. Although
this will take you some time, it
is worth the effort as the soup
will be smoother.*

Drain the chick-peas and rinse under cold water. Cook them in plenty of boiling water for 1–1½ hours until tender. Drain and peel (see Cook's Tip).

Place the onion and parsley in a blender or food processor and blend until finely chopped. Alternatively, chop each very finely and mix together. Heat the olive and sunflower oils in a saucepan or flameproof casserole and fry the onion mixture for 3–4 minutes over a low heat until the onion is slightly softened. Add the chick-peas, cook gently for 1–2 minutes and add the stock. Season well with salt and pepper. Bring the soup to the boil, then cover and simmer for 20 minutes until the chick-peas are very tender.

Allow the soup to cool a little and then part-purée in a blender or food processor, or mash with a fork, so that the soup is thick but still chunky.

Return the soup to a clean pan, add the lemon juice and adjust the seasoning if necessary. Heat gently and then serve garnished with lemon wedges and finely pared rind, and accompanied by crusty bread.

CEP SOUP WITH PARSLEY CROUTONS

The little parsley croûtons add a mild, herby flavour to this delicious and unusual soup.

Serves 4

50g/2oz/4 tbsp butter

2 onions, finely chopped

1 garlic clove

225g/8oz fresh ceps or button
    mushrooms, trimmed and sliced

75ml/5 tbsp dry white wine

900ml/1½ pints/3¾ cups boiling
    chicken stock

115g/4oz floury potatoes, peeled
    and diced

1 thyme sprig

15ml/1 tbsp lemon juice

salt and freshly ground black pepper

For the parsley croûtons

50g/2oz/4 tbsp butter

3 slices day-old bread, cut into
    2.5cm/1in fingers

45ml/3 tbsp finely chopped fresh
    parsley

Melt the butter in a large saucepan and fry the onions for 4–5 minutes until lightly browned. Add the garlic, mushrooms and wine, stir briefly then add the stock, potatoes and thyme. Simmer gently for 45 minutes.

Pour the soup into a blender or food processor and blend briefly so that pieces of mushroom are left intact. Transfer the soup to a clean pan, add the lemon juice and season to taste.

Make the croûtons. Melt the butter in a large frying pan and add the fingers of bread. Fry for 2–3 minutes until golden and then stir in the parsley. Ladle the soup into warmed soup bowls, add the parsley croûtons and serve.

SALSA VERDE

This is a classic salsa, made with chillies, onions and plenty of fresh parsley.

Serves 4

2–4 green chillies, seeded

8 spring onions, trimmed and halved

2 garlic cloves, halved

50g/2oz salted capers

fresh tarragon sprig

40g/1½oz fresh parsley

grated rind and juice of 1 lime

90ml/6 tbsp olive oil

about 15ml/1 tbsp green Tabasco sauce, to taste

freshly ground black pepper

COOK'S TIP

If you can only find capers pickled in vinegar, rinse well in cold water before using.

Place the chillies, spring onions and garlic in a blender or food processor and blend briefly until the ingredients are roughly chopped. Rub the excess salt off the capers, but do not rinse them. Add the capers to the chilli and onion mixture, together with the tarragon and parsley. Blend again until finely chopped.

Transfer the mixture to a small bowl and stir in the lime rind and juice and olive oil. Stir briefly to mix. Add the green Tabasco sauce and black pepper. Chill in the fridge until ready to serve, but do not prepare more than 8 hours in advance.

GRILLED PARSLEY MUSSELS

This is a really great tapas dish. The parsley and Parmesan make a fantastic topping and you'll find they are devoured the moment they are ready!

Serves 4

450g/1lb fresh mussels

15ml/1 tbsp melted butter

15ml/1 tbsp olive oil

45ml/3 tbsp freshly grated Parmesan cheese

30ml/2 tbsp chopped fresh parsley

2 garlic cloves, finely chopped

2.5ml/½ tsp coarsely ground black pepper

Scrub the mussels thoroughly, pulling away the gritty beards. Discard any mussels that don't close when sharply tapped with a knife.

Place the mussels and 45ml/3 tbsp water in a large pan. Cover and steam for 5–6 minutes until all the mussels have opened. Drain, discarding any that remain closed.

Remove and discard the top shell of each mussel. Place the mussels in a flameproof dish, packing them closely together so that they stay level. Preheat the grill to high.

Mix together the melted butter, olive oil, Parmesan, parsley, garlic and black pepper. Spoon a little of this mixture on top of each mussel and grill for 2–3 minutes until the mussels are sizzling and golden. Serve the mussels in their shells.

COOK'S TIP

This is a dish to serve to good friends as it can be rather messy! Remember to give guests napkins to wipe the juices off their chins.

OMELETTE AUX FINES HERBES

Parsley, chervil, chives and tarragon are the four traditional ingredients in French fines herbes. This omelette is a classic favourite and makes a welcome snack for lunch or supper.

Serves 1

3 eggs
30ml/2 tbsp chopped fresh parsley
30ml/2 tbsp chopped fresh chervil
30ml/2 tbsp chopped fresh tarragon
15ml/1 tbsp chopped fresh chives
15ml/¹⁄₂oz/1 tbsp butter
salt and freshly ground black pepper
chips, green salad and tomato,
*   to serve*

COOK'S TIP
From start to finish, an omelette should be cooked and on the table in less than a minute. For best results, use free-range eggs at room temperature.

Beat the eggs with a little salt and pepper and then whisk in the chopped parsley, chervil, tarragon and chives.

Heat an omelette or frying pan over a high heat and add the butter. When the butter begins to foam and brown, quickly pour in the beaten egg and stir briskly with a fork. When the egg is two-thirds scrambled, let the omelette finish cooking for a further 10–15 seconds.

Fold the omelette on to a warmed serving plate. Serve with chips, green salad and a halved tomato.

PARSLEY AND GARLIC MUSHROOMS

Mushrooms, parsley and garlic have a long and happy association. The lemon juice adds a pleasant sharpness to this dish, tempering the garlic and bringing out the flavour of the parsley.

Serves 4

25g/1oz/2 tbsp butter, plus extra for
  spreading
1 onion, finely chopped
1 garlic clove, crushed
350g/12oz assorted wild and
  cultivated mushrooms, sliced
45ml/3 tbsp dry sherry
75ml/5 tbsp chopped fresh flat leaf
  parsley
15ml/1 tbsp lemon juice
salt and freshly ground black pepper
4 slices brown or white bread

Melt the butter in a large non-stick frying pan and gently fry the onion until softened but not browned. Add the garlic and mushrooms, cover and cook for 3–5 minutes. Add the sherry and cook, uncovered, for a further 2–3 minutes until the liquid has evaporated.

Stir in the parsley and lemon juice and season to taste. Toast the bread and spread with butter. Spoon the mushrooms over the toast and serve.

COOK'S TIP
Wild mushrooms are becoming available in larger supermarkets or you may be lucky enough to have your own supply. Field mushrooms, shaggy ink caps and orange birch boletes are all excellent in this dish.

23

MACKEREL AND PARSLEY PATE

Parsley adds flavour and colour to this popular pâté. Serve it as a simple starter or snack with chicory leaves and fingers of toast.

Serves 4

275g/10oz smoked mackerel fillet, skinned

90ml/6 tbsp soured cream

75g/3oz/6 tbsp butter, softened

30ml/2 tbsp chopped fresh parsley

15–30ml/1–2 tbsp lemon juice

freshly ground black pepper

chicory leaves and parsley, to garnish

fingers of toast, to serve

Remove any skin or bones from the mackerel and then mash it with a fork. Add the soured cream and butter, blending to make a smooth paste. Stir in the parsley, lemon juice and pepper to taste.

Spoon the pâté into a dish or bowl, cover with clear film and chill overnight.

About 30 minutes before serving, remove the pâté from the fridge and allow it to return to room temperature. To serve, spoon on to individual plates and garnish with chicory leaves and parsley. Serve with fingers of toast.

COOK'S TIP

For a lower-calorie version of this pâté, substitute 200g/ 7oz/scant 1 cup low-fat soft cheese or sieved cottage cheese for the soured cream.

POTTED STILTON WITH PARSLEY

The parsley and chives give this appetizing starter a great country-style flavour. It is best made the day before so that the herbs and port can blend with the Stilton. Serve with crispy Melba toast.

Serves 8

225g/8oz blue Stilton or other blue
  cheese
115g/4oz/1/4 cup full- or half-fat
  cream cheese
15ml/1 tbsp port
15ml/1 tbsp chopped fresh parsley
15ml/1 tbsp snipped fresh chives, plus
  extra to garnish
50g/2oz/1/2 cup finely chopped
  walnuts
salt and freshly ground black pepper

For the Melba toast
12 thin slices white bread

COOK'S TIP
Take care when making Melba toast. It burns very quickly – so watch it constantly.

Place the Stilton or other blue cheese, cream cheese and port in a blender or food processor and blend until smooth. Add the parsley, chives and walnuts and season to taste with salt and pepper.

Spoon the mixture into individual ramekin dishes and level the tops. Cover with clear film and chill, preferably overnight.

Just before serving, make the Melba toast. Heat the grill and toast the bread on both sides. While the toast is still hot, cut off the crusts and cut each slice horizontally in two. Place the bread in a single layer on a grill pan and grill for about 30 seconds until golden brown and crisp.

Sprinkle the potted cheese with chives and serve with Melba toast.

Meat and Poultry

Parsley enlivens stuffings and coatings and is great with all meats and poultry. From Russia, through Morocco to England, parsley has a place in every kitchen.

BEEF STROGANOFF WITH PARSLEY

Parsley is one of the traditional ingredients in this famous nineteenth-century Russian recipe.

Serves 4

*450g/1lb fillet or rump steak,
    trimmed and cut into thin strips*
30ml/2 tbsp olive oil
45ml/3 tbsp brandy
2 shallots, finely chopped
*225g/8oz chanterelle or button
    mushrooms, trimmed and halved*
150ml/¼ pint/⅔ cup beef stock
75ml/5 tbsp soured cream
5ml/1 tsp Dijon mustard
½ gherkin, chopped
45ml/3 tbsp chopped fresh parsley
salt and freshly ground black pepper
*buttered noodles and poppy seeds,
    to serve*

COOK'S TIP
*To flame the brandy, heat
quickly, stand back from the
pan and then tilt the pan
towards the flame, or ignite with
a match if cooking on an
electric hob.*

Season the steak with pepper. Heat half the oil in a frying pan and fry the steak for 2 minutes until evenly browned. Transfer to a large plate. Heat the pan over a moderately high heat, brown the sediment, then add the brandy and ignite the alcohol vapour. Wait until the flames subside and then pour the juices over the meat. Keep warm.

Wipe the pan and fry the shallots in the remaining oil for about 2 minutes. Add the mushrooms and fry gently for 3–4 minutes to soften. Stir in the stock and simmer for a few minutes, then add the soured cream, mustard and gherkin together with the steak and its juices. Simmer briefly, season to taste and stir in the chopped parsley. Serve with buttered noodles sprinkled with poppy seeds.

27

BEEF WELLINGTON

The parsley pancakes make an unusual and tasty addition to this popular dish. The traditional goose liver pâté is replaced here with a rich mushroom pâté.

Serves 4

675g/1½lb fillet steak, tied

15ml/1 tbsp sunflower oil

350g/12oz puff pastry, thawed if
   frozen

1 egg, beaten, to glaze

salt and freshly ground black pepper

watercress, to garnish

For the parsley pancakes

50g/2oz/4 tbsp plain flour

1 egg

150ml/¼ pint/⅔ cup milk

30ml/2 tbsp chopped fresh parsley

For the mushroom pâté

50g/2oz/1 cup fresh white
   breadcrumbs

75ml/5 tbsp double cream

2 egg yolks

25g/1oz/2 tbsp butter

2 shallots or 1 small onion, chopped

450g/1lb assorted wild and
   cultivated mushrooms, chopped

Preheat the oven to 220°C/425°F/Gas 7 and season the meat with black pepper. Heat the oil in a roasting tin, add the meat and brown on all sides. Transfer to the oven and roast for 15 minutes for rare, 20 minutes for medium-rare and 25 minutes for well-done meat. Set aside to cool. Reduce the oven temperature to 190°C/375°F/Gas 5.

Make the pancakes. Beat together the flour, a pinch of salt, the egg, milk and parsley to make a smooth batter. Heat a large non-stick frying pan and pour in enough batter to coat the bottom. When set, flip over and cook briefly until lightly browned. Continue with the remaining batter to make four pancakes.

Make the mushroom pâté. Blend together the breadcrumbs, cream and egg yolks. Melt the butter in a frying pan and fry the shallots or onion until slightly softened. Add the mushrooms and cook briskly until the juices begin to run and then evaporate. When the mushrooms are quite dry, stir in the breadcrumb mixture, blending to make a smooth paste. Allow to cool.

Roll out the pastry and cut into a rectangle 35 x 30cm/14 x 12in. Place two pancakes on the pastry and spread with mushroom pâté. Place the beef on top and spread over any remaining pâté. Cover with the remaining pancakes. Cut out four small squares from the corners of the pastry and reserve. Moisten the pastry edges and wrap over the meat.

Decorate the top with the reserved pastry trimming and transfer to a baking sheet. Brush the pastry evenly with beaten egg and cook for about 40 minutes until golden brown. Serve garnished with watercress.

SHISH KEBAB

This is one of the most famous dishes of the Arab world and it is cooked with lots of fresh parsley. Lamb is the traditional Moroccan meat for this dish, although beef can be used.

Serves 4

675g/1½lb lamb or beef

1 onion, grated

30ml/2 tbsp chopped fresh flat leaf parsley

5ml/1 tsp paprika

5ml/1 tsp ground cumin

15ml/1 tbsp olive oil

15ml/1 tbsp lemon juice

salt and freshly ground black pepper

fine strips of lemon rind and chopped fresh parsley, to garnish

Moroccan bread, lemon wedges, cumin seeds and cayenne pepper, to serve

COOK'S TIP

Moroccan cooks often intersperse lamb or beef fat with the meat, which adds flavour and keeps the meat moist. Alternatively, if using lamb, choose a more fatty cut.

Cut the meat into fairly small pieces, measuring approximately 2cm/¾in square. Mix the grated onion, parsley, paprika, cumin, oil, lemon juice and seasoning in a large bowl and add the meat. Stir so that the meat is coated thoroughly, then set aside for about 2 hours.

Prepare a barbecue or preheat the grill. Thread the meat on to metal skewers, allowing about six to eight pieces of meat per skewer. Grill or barbecue the meat a few centimetres from the heat for 6–8 minutes or until the meat is cooked through, basting occasionally with the marinade. Arrange the kebabs on a serving plate and garnish with fine strips of lemon rind and chopped fresh parsley. Serve with Moroccan bread, lemon wedges and dishes of cumin seeds and cayenne pepper.

PORK WITH PARSLEY DUMPLINGS

The parsley dumplings really give this rich stew a country-style flavour. The pork is cooked with prunes and apricots – a delicious fruity combination that goes beautifully with this meat.

Serves 6

115g/4oz/½ cup pitted prunes,
   roughly chopped
115g/4oz/½ cup dried apricots,
   roughly chopped
300ml/½ pint/1¼ cups dry cider
30ml/2 tbsp plain flour
675g/1½lb lean boneless pork, cubed
about 30ml/2 tbsp sunflower oil
2 onions, roughly chopped
2 garlic cloves, crushed
6 celery sticks, roughly chopped
475ml/16fl oz/2 cups chicken stock
12 juniper berries, lightly crushed
30ml/2 tbsp chopped fresh thyme
425g/15oz can black-eyed beans,
   drained
salt and freshly ground black pepper

For the parsley dumplings

115g/4oz/1 cup self-raising flour
50g/2oz/generous ⅓ cup vegetable
   suet
45ml/3 tbsp chopped fresh parsley

Soak the prunes and apricots in the cider for 20 minutes. Preheat the oven to 180°C/350°F/Gas 4. Season the flour with salt and pepper and dust the pork cubes, reserving any left-over flour. Heat the oil in a large flameproof casserole and brown the meat in batches, adding a little more oil if necessary. Transfer to a plate with a slotted spoon.

Add the onions, garlic and celery to the casserole and cook for 5–6 minutes until the vegetables are slightly softened, stirring occasionally. Add the reserved flour and cook, stirring, for 1 minute. Blend in the stock, stirring until smooth, then add the dried fruit and cider, juniper berries, thyme and seasoning. Bring to the boil and add the pork. Cover and cook in the oven for 50 minutes.

Just before the end of cooking, prepare the dumplings. Sift the flour into a bowl and stir in the suet and parsley. Add about 90ml/6 tbsp water and stir to make a dough. Form into six dumplings.

Stir the beans into the casserole and adjust the seasoning. Arrange the dumplings on the stew, cover and cook in the oven for a further 20–25 minutes until the dumplings are puffy and the pork is tender.

PARSLEY-CRUSTED LAMB

Parsley and oatmeal make a wonderful crunchy coating for this elegant and succulent dish.

Serves 6

*2 best-end necks of lamb, about
1kg/2¼lb each*

finely grated rind of 1 lemon

60ml/4 tbsp medium oatmeal

*50g/2oz/1 cup fresh white
breadcrumbs*

*60ml/4 tbsp chopped fresh flat leaf
parsley*

25g/1oz/2 tbsp butter, melted

30ml/2 tbsp clear honey

salt and freshly ground black pepper

fresh parsley sprigs, to garnish

roasted baby vegetables, to serve

COOK'S TIP

*Ask the butcher to remove the
chine bone for you, which will
make carving easier. Racks of
lamb sold in supermarkets are
normally "chined" already.*

Preheat the oven to 200°C/400°F/Gas 6. Trim the racks of lamb so that about 2.5cm/1in bone at the top is exposed. Trim the skin and some of the fat from the outer side of the rack and score with a sharp knife.

Mix together the lemon rind, oatmeal, breadcrumbs, chopped parsley and seasoning and stir in the melted butter. Brush the fatty side of each rack with honey and press the oatmeal mixture evenly over the surface.

Place the racks in a roasting tin with the oatmeal sides uppermost. Roast for 40–50 minutes, depending on whether you like rare or medium lamb. Cover loosely with foil if browning too much. To serve, slice each rack into three and arrange on warmed serving plates with roasted vegetables, garnished with parsley sprigs.

CHICKEN WITH PARSLEY STUFFING

These little chicken drumsticks have a delectable herby flavour, in which parsley predominates.

Serves 4

60ml/4 tbsp ricotta cheese

1 garlic clove, crushed

30ml/2 tbsp chopped fresh parsley

15ml/1 tbsp mixed chopped fresh
chives and tarragon

5ml/1 tsp mint

30ml/2 tbsp fresh brown
breadcrumbs

8 chicken drumsticks

8 smoked streaky bacon rashers

5ml/1 tsp wholegrain mustard

15ml/1 tbsp sunflower oil

salt and freshly ground black pepper

chopped fresh parsley and chives,
to garnish

COOK'S TIP

If, thanks to the elements, you
can't use the barbecue, cook
indoors in the oven at 180°C/
350°F/Gas 4 for 25–30
minutes, turning occasionally.

Mix together the ricotta, garlic, herbs, breadcrumbs and seasoning. Carefully loosen the skin of each drumstick and spoon a little of the herb stuffing under the skin. Smooth the skin firmly over the stuffing.

Wrap a bacon rasher around the wide end of each drumstick, to hold the skin in place over the stuffing.

Mix together the mustard and oil and brush over the chicken. Cook over a medium-hot barbecue for about 25 minutes, turning occasionally, until the chicken is cooked through and the meat juices run clear. Serve garnished with chopped parsley and chives.

CHICKEN FRICASSEE FORESTIER

Chicken, wild mushrooms and lashings of parsley make this a truly splendid dish, perfect for a special meal, yet surprisingly easy and quick to make.

Serves 4

3 boned chicken breasts, sliced
15ml/1 tbsp sunflower oil
50g/2oz/4 tbsp butter
115g/4oz unsmoked streaky bacon, chopped
75ml/5 tbsp dry sherry or white wine
1 onion, chopped
350g/12oz assorted wild and cultivated mushrooms, sliced
40g/1½oz/3 tbsp plain flour
500ml/18fl oz/2¼ cups chicken stock
10ml/2 tsp lemon juice
60ml/4 tbsp chopped fresh parsley
salt and freshly ground black pepper
boiled rice, carrots and baby sweetcorn, to serve

COOK'S TIP
It is worth spending a little extra on free-range chicken for the low fat content and good flavour and texture of the meat.

Season the chicken with a little pepper. Heat the oil and half of the butter in a large frying pan or flameproof casserole and brown the chicken and bacon pieces. Transfer to a dish and pour off any excess fat. Return the pan to the heat and brown the sediment. Pour in the sherry or wine, stir with a wooden spoon to deglaze the pan and then pour the liquid over the chicken. Wipe the pan clean.

Fry the onion in the remaining butter until golden brown. Add the mushrooms and cook, stirring frequently, for 6–8 minutes. Reduce the heat, stir in the flour and then gradually add the chicken stock, stirring to make a smooth sauce.

Add the reserved chicken and bacon together with the sherry juices and heat until simmering. Simmer for 10–15 minutes until the chicken is cooked, then add the lemon juice, parsley (reserve a little parsley to scatter over the rice if you wish) and seasoning. Serve with plain boiled rice, carrots and baby sweetcorn.

CHICKEN, LEEK AND PARSLEY PIE

This is a classic English country dish. The creamy parsley sauce is the perfect complement to the chicken and leeks, bound together in an exquisite whole with wonderful melt-in-the-mouth pastry.

Serves 4–6

3 part-boned chicken breasts
flavouring ingredients (bouquet
*   garni, black peppercorns, onion*
*   and carrot)*
50g/2oz/4 tbsp butter
2 leeks, thinly sliced
50g/2oz/½ cup Cheddar cheese,
*   grated*
25g/1oz/⅓ cup Parmesan cheese,
*   grated*
45ml/3 tbsp chopped fresh parsley
30ml/2 tbsp wholegrain mustard
5ml/1 tsp cornflour
300ml/½ pint/1¼ cups double cream
salt and freshly ground black pepper
beaten egg, to glaze
mixed green salad, to serve

For the pastry
275g/10oz/2½ cups plain flour
200g/7oz/scant 1 cup butter, diced
2 egg yolks
pinch of salt

Make the pastry. Sift the flour and salt into a bowl. Blend the butter and egg yolks in a food processor until creamy. Add the flour and process very briefly until the mixture is just coming together. Add about 15ml/1 tbsp cold water and process for a few seconds more. Turn out on to a lightly floured surface and knead lightly. Wrap in clear film and chill for about 1 hour.

Meanwhile, place the chicken breasts in a single layer in a frying pan. Add the flavouring ingredients and enough water to just cover. Cover the pan with a lid and simmer very gently for about 20–25 minutes until the chicken is tender. Leave to cool in the liquid.

Preheat the oven to 200°C/400°F/Gas 6. Divide the pastry into two pieces, one slightly larger than the other. Roll out the larger piece on a lightly floured surface and use to line a 28 x 18cm/11 x 7in baking dish or tin. Prick the base with a fork and bake in the oven for 15 minutes. Leave to cool.

Discard the skin and bones from the chicken and cut the flesh into strips. Melt the butter in a frying pan and fry the leeks over a low heat until soft, stirring occasionally. Stir in the cheeses and parsley. Spead half the leek mixture over the cooked pastry base, cover with the chicken strips and then top with the remaining leek mixture. Mix together the mustard, cornflour and cream in a small bowl. Add seasoning to taste and pour over the filling.

Moisten the edges of the cooked pastry base. Roll out the remaining pastry and cover the pie. Brush with beaten egg and bake in the oven for 30–40 minutes until crisp and golden. Serve hot with a mixed green salad.

Fish and Seafood

Its mild, pleasant flavour makes parsley
an essential ingredient when cooking with fish.
Sauces, risottos and tasty fish soups would be
incomplete without this fresh green herb.

FISH STEW WITH PARSLEY

This rustic stew harbours all sorts of tantalizing flavours, enhanced by aromatic flat leaf parsley.

Serves 4

1kg/2¼lb assorted white fish fillets

*225g/8oz button mushrooms, halved
  if large*

225g/8oz canned tomatoes

450ml/¾ pint/1¾ cups dry cider

10ml/2 tsp plain flour

15ml/1 tbsp butter

45ml/3 tbsp Calvados

*15ml/1 tbsp chopped fresh flat leaf
  parsley*

15ml/1 tbsp chopped fresh dill

salt and freshly ground black pepper

*flat leaf parsley sprigs and dill,
  to garnish*

Preheat the oven to 180°C/350°F/Gas 4. Chop the fish roughly and place in a casserole with the mushrooms and tomatoes. Heat the cider in a small pan. Work the flour into the butter and stir, bit by bit, into the cider to make a smooth sauce. Remove the pan from the heat.

Stir in the Calvados, chopped parsley and dill and season to taste with salt and pepper. Pour into the casserole with the fish and mushrooms, cover and cook in the oven for about 30 minutes until the fish is tender. Serve garnished with parsley sprigs and dill.

CRAB CAKES WITH PARSLEY SAUCE

These crab cakes are served with a tartar-like sauce, richly flavoured with onions, capers and parsley.

Serves 4

675g/1½lb fresh crab meat

1 egg, beaten

30ml/2 tbsp mayonnaise

15ml/1 tbsp Worcestershire sauce

15ml/1 tbsp dry sherry

*30ml/2 tbsp finely chopped fresh
parsley*

*15ml/1 tbsp finely chopped fresh
chives or dill*

45ml/3 tbsp olive oil

salt and freshly ground black pepper

*chives, slices of lemon and salad
leaves, to garnish*

For the parsley sauce

1 egg yolk

15ml/1 tbsp white wine vinegar

30ml/2 tbsp Dijon mustard

250ml/8fl oz/1 cup sunflower oil

30ml/2 tbsp lemon juice

2 spring onions, finely chopped

30ml/2 tbsp drained capers, chopped

3–4 gherkins, finely chopped

45ml/3 tbsp chopped fresh parsley

Place the crab meat in a bowl, discarding any pieces of shell but keeping the pieces of crab as large as possible.

Put the egg, mayonnaise, Worcestershire sauce, sherry and chopped herbs in a bowl and stir to mix. Season with salt and pepper, then fold in the crab meat. Divide the mixture into eight oval cakes and place on a baking sheet between layers of greaseproof paper. Chill for at least 1 hour.

Meanwhile, make the sauce. Using a wire whisk, beat the egg yolk and add the vinegar, mustard and seasoning. Whisk in the oil, at first drop by drop and then in a slow, steady stream, to make a smooth mayonnaise. Add the lemon juice, spring onions, capers, gherkins and parsley and mix well. Adjust the seasoning, cover and chill.

Preheat the grill. Brush the crab cakes with the olive oil and place on an oiled baking sheet. Grill under a moderately hot heat for about 5 minutes each side until golden brown. Serve hot with the parsley sauce, garnished with chives, lemon slices and a few salad leaves.

SEAFOOD RISOTTO WITH PARSLEY

Parsley and chervil add colour and a pleasant, aromatic flavour to this tasty risotto. Use short-grain Arborio rice which has a creamy texture to complement the shellfish and mushrooms.

Serves 4

225g/8oz fresh mussels

45ml/3 tbsp olive oil

1 onion, chopped

225g/8oz assorted wild and cultivated
   mushrooms, trimmed and sliced

450g/1lb/2¼ cups short-grain
   Arborio rice

1.2 litres/2 pints/5 cups boiling
   chicken or vegetable stock

150ml/¼ pint/⅔ cup white wine

115g/4oz raw prawns, peeled

225g/8oz clams

1 squid, cleaned, trimmed and sliced

75ml/5 tbsp mixed chopped fresh flat
   leaf parsley and chervil

celery salt and cayenne pepper

COOK'S TIP

Be sure to discard any uncooked mussels that do not close when sharply tapped.

Scrub the mussels thoroughly, pulling away the gritty beards. Discard any mussels that don't close when sharply tapped with a knife. Heat the oil in a large frying pan and fry the onion for 6–8 minutes until softened but not browned. Add the mushrooms and cook for 5–6 minutes, stirring occasionally. Add the rice and cook for about 1 minute to coat the rice in oil, then pour in the stock and wine. Add the prawns, mussels, clams and squid and simmer for 15 minutes, stirring occasionally. Discard any shellfish that have not opened during cooking.

Add the herbs, stir well, then remove from the heat. Cover tightly and allow to stand for 5–10 minutes until the rice is completely tender. Season with celery salt and cayenne pepper to taste, and serve.

PARSLEY-STUFFED PLAICE ROLLS

Sun-dried tomatoes, pine nuts and plenty of flat leaf parsley make an appetizing stuffing with a superb southern European flavour.

Serves 4

4 plaice fillets, about 225g/8oz each,
  skinned
75g/3oz/6 tbsp butter
1 small onion, chopped
1 celery stick, finely chopped
115g/4oz/2 cups fresh white
  breadcrumbs
45ml/3 tbsp chopped fresh flat leaf
  parsley
30ml/2 tbsp pine nuts, toasted
3 – 4 sun-dried tomatoes in oil,
  drained and chopped
50g/2oz can anchovy fillets, drained
  and chopped
75ml/5 tbsp hot fish stock
freshly ground black pepper

> ### COOK'S TIP
> *This dish is superb served with baby new potatoes topped with a knob of butter.*

Preheat the oven to 180°C/350°F/Gas 4. Using a sharp knife, cut the plaice fillets in half lengthways to make eight smaller fillets. Melt the butter in a pan. Add the onion and celery and cook, covered, over a very gentle heat for about 15 minutes until they are both very soft. Mix together the breadcrumbs, parsley, pine nuts, sun-dried tomatoes and anchovies in a bowl. Stir in the softened vegetables and buttery juices and season with freshly ground black pepper.

Divide the stuffing into eight portions and form each one into a small ball. Roll this up inside a plaice fillet, securing each roll with a cocktail stick.

Place the rolled-up fillets in a buttered ovenproof dish. Pour over the fish stock, cover with buttered foil and bake for about 20 minutes until the fish flakes easily. Remove the cocktail sticks and serve with a little of the cooking juices drizzled over.

HADDOCK AND PARSLEY SAUCE

Parsley sauce is a classic with white fish but it is excellent with smoked fish too. Add lots of parsley and season well so that the sauce stands up to the smoky flavour of the fish.

Serves 4

4 smoked haddock fillets, about
*   225g/8oz each*
75g/3oz/6 tbsp butter, softened
25g/1oz/2 tbsp plain flour
300ml/½ pint/1¼ cups milk
60ml/4 tbsp chopped fresh parsley
salt and freshly ground black pepper
fresh parsley sprigs, to garnish

COOK'S TIP
You could use flat leaf or curly parsley for this dish. Flat leaf parsley has the more aromatic flavour but curly parsley is also very good and would be the traditional variety to serve with this British dish.

Smear the fish fillets on both sides with 50g/2oz/4 tbsp of the butter and preheat the grill. Beat the remaining butter and flour together to make a thick paste.

Grill the fish for 10–15 minutes, turning when necessary. Meanwhile, heat the milk until just below boiling point. Add the flour mixture in small pieces, whisking constantly over the heat. Continue until you have used all the flour mixture and the sauce is smooth and thick.

Stir in the parsley and season well to taste. Pour over the fish, garnish with parsley and serve.

DOVER SOLE IN A PARSLEY JACKET

Quick to prepare and absolutely delicious, there is nothing to compare with the rich sweetness of Dover sole. The parsley adds a subtle flavour as well as looking magnificent.

Serves 2

2 Dover sole, skinned

25g/1oz/2 tbsp butter

salt and freshly ground black pepper

lemon wedges, halved cherry
*   tomatoes and fresh flat leaf parsley*
*   sprigs, to garnish*

mashed potatoes, to serve

For the parsley jacket

25g/1oz fresh flat leaf parsley

25g/1oz crustless white bread, cubed

45ml/3 tbsp milk

30ml/2 tbsp olive oil

finely grated rind of 1/2 small lemon

2 small garlic cloves, crushed

First make the parsley jacket. Place the parsley in a food processor and process until finely chopped. Add the bread, milk, olive oil, lemon rind and garlic and process to make a fine paste.

Preheat a moderate grill. Season the fish, dot with butter and grill for 5 minutes. Turn and grill for 2 minutes on the other side. Spread this side with the parsley mixture and cook under the grill for a further 5 minutes until the fish flakes easily. Garnish the fish with lemon wedges, tomato halves and parsley and serve with creamy mashed potatoes.

SPANISH-STYLE HAKE WITH PARSLEY

This is essentially a main meal soup. Fish, mussels and green beans make the substance of the soup while the stock is flavoured with wine, sherry and lots of lovely parsley.

Serves 4

16–20 fresh mussels

30ml/2 tbsp olive oil

25g/1oz/2 tbsp butter

1 onion, chopped

3 garlic cloves, crushed

15ml/1 tbsp plain flour

2.5ml/½ tsp paprika

4 hake cutlets, about 175g/6oz each

225g/8oz fine green beans, cut into

*   2.5cm/1in lengths*

350ml/12fl oz/1½ cups fish stock

150ml/¼ pint/⅔ cup dry white wine

30ml/2 tbsp dry sherry

45ml/3 tbsp chopped fresh parsley

salt and freshly ground black pepper

crusty bread, to serve

COOK'S TIP
*Cod and haddock cutlets
will work just as well in this
tasty dish.*

Scrub the mussels thoroughly, pulling away the gritty beards. Discard any mussels that don't close when sharply tapped with a knife. Heat the oil and butter in a frying pan and fry the onion for 5 minutes until softened but not browned. Add the crushed garlic and cook for a further 1 minute.

Mix together the flour and paprika and lightly dust the hake cutlets. Push the onion and garlic to one side of the pan and add the fish. Fry on both sides until golden, then carefully stir in the beans, stock, wine, sherry and seasoning. Bring to the boil and cook for about 2 minutes.

Add the prepared mussels and parsley, cover the pan and cook for 5–8 minutes until the mussels have opened. Discard any mussels that remain closed.

Serve this dish in warmed, shallow soup bowls with crusty bread to mop up the juices.

Vegetable Dishes

Parsley is the perfect herb for subtle vegetable
dishes. Whether used in sauces, stirred into
stuffings or starring in salads, this versatile herb
adds vibrant colour with its unassuming but
much-loved flavour.

STUFFED PARSLEY ONIONS

The tasty parsley stuffing goes perfectly with roasted onions. Serve as part of a vegetarian meal or as an accompaniment to roast meat or chicken.

Serves 4

4 large onions

60ml/4 tbsp cooked rice

20ml/4 tsp finely chopped fresh
  parsley, plus extra to garnish

60ml/4 tbsp grated Chedddar cheese

30ml/2 tbsp olive oil

about 15ml/1 tbsp white wine,
  to moisten

salt and freshly ground black pepper

COOK'S TIP

The onion centres can be used in soups or for other dishes. However, uncooked cut onion does not keep well, so use on the same day or discard.

Preheat the oven to 180°C/350°F/Gas 4. Cut a slice from the top of each onion and scoop out the centre, leaving a fairly thick shell. Blend together the cooked rice, parsley, cheese, olive oil and seasoning, moistening with enough wine to mix well.

Fill the onions and bake in the oven for 45 minutes. Serve garnished with a sprinkling of chopped parsley.

PARSLEYED VEGETABLE RIBBONS

Brie and parsley combine to make a delicately flavoured sauce to serve with these elegant vegetables.

Serves 4

15ml/1 tbsp sunflower oil

1 large green pepper, cored and diced

225g/8oz Brie cheese

30ml/2 tbsp crème fraîche

5ml/1 tsp lemon juice

60ml/4 tbsp milk

10ml/2 tsp freshly ground black pepper

2–3 fresh parsley sprigs

6 large courgettes

6 large carrots

chopped fresh parsley, to garnish

Heat the oil in a pan and sauté the green pepper for 4–5 minutes until just tender. Place the Brie, crème fraîche, lemon juice, milk, black pepper and parsley sprigs in a food processor and blend well. Add the mixture to the green pepper and heat gently.

Using a potato peeler, slice the courgettes and carrots into thin strips. Place them in separate saucepans with enough water to cover and simmer for 3 minutes until just tender. The courgettes will take 2–3 minutes, the carrots a little longer. Drain.

Pour the warm sauce into a shallow serving dish. Add the courgettes and carrots and toss carefully to coat in the sauce. Garnish with a little finely chopped parsley and serve.

LEEKS WITH PARSLEY DRESSING

The parsley dressing gives these leeks a wonderful flavour. Serve French-style as a salade tiède *(warm salad), with grilled or poached fish and new potatoes.*

Serves 4
700g/1½lb young leeks

For the dressing
25g/1oz fresh flat leaf parsley
30ml/2 tbsp olive oil
juice of ½ lemon
50g/2oz/½ cup broken walnuts,
  toasted
5ml/1 tsp caster sugar
1 hard-boiled egg, shelled
salt and freshly ground black pepper

Cut the leeks into 10cm/4in lengths and rinse well to remove any grit or soil. Bring a saucepan of salted water to the boil and simmer the leeks for 8 minutes. Drain and rinse in cold water to cool slightly and then drain again thoroughly.

Make the dressing. Reserve a sprig or two of parsley for the garnish and put the remainder in a blender or food processor. Blend until finely chopped, add the olive oil, lemon juice and toasted walnuts and blend again for 1–2 minutes until smooth. Add about 90ml/6 tbsp water to make a smooth sauce and add sugar and seasoning to taste.

Arrange the leeks on a serving plate and spoon over the sauce. Finely grate the hard-boiled egg and scatter over the sauce. Serve at room temperature, garnished with the reserved parsley.

PARSLEY AND ARTICHOKE CREPES

Fill thin pancakes with a mouth-watering soufflé mixture of Jerusalem artichokes, leeks and freshly chopped parsley to serve for a special main course.

Serves 4

115g/4oz/1 cup plain flour

pinch of salt

1 egg

300ml/¹/₂ pint/1¹/₄ cups milk

For the soufflé filling

450g/1lb Jerusalem artichokes, peeled
*   and diced*

1 large leek, thinly sliced

50g/2oz/4 tbsp butter

30ml/2 tbsp self-raising flour

30ml/2 tbsp single cream

75g/3oz Cheddar cheese, grated

30ml/2 tbsp fresh parsley, chopped

fresh nutmeg, grated

2 eggs, separated

COOK'S TIP

Make sure the pan is at a good steady heat and is well oiled before you pour in the batter. It should sizzle as it hits the pan.

Make the crêpe batter. Blend the flour, salt, egg and milk to a smooth batter in a food processor or blender. Using a crêpe or omelette pan with a diameter of about 20cm/8in, make a batch of thin pancakes. You will need about 30ml/2 tbsp of batter for each one. Stack the pancakes under a tea towel as you make them. Reserve eight for this dish and freeze the rest.

Cook the artichokes and leek with the butter in a covered saucepan on a gentle heat for about 12 minutes until very soft. Mash with the back of a wooden spoon. Season well. Stir the flour into the vegetables and cook for 1 minute more. Take the pan off the heat and beat in the cream, cheese, parsley and nutmeg. Season to taste. Cool, then add the egg yolks.

Whisk the egg whites until they form soft peaks and carefully fold them into the leek and artichoke mixture. Lightly grease a small ovenproof dish and preheat the oven to 190°C/375°F/Gas 5. Fold each pancake in four, hold the top open and spoon the mixture into the centre. Arrange the crêpes in the prepared dish with the filling uppermost if possible. Bake for about 15 minutes until risen and golden. Serve immediately.

BEANS WITH PARSLEY SAUCE

In this classic dish the parsley sauce is enriched with egg yolks and double cream.

Serves 4

20g/³⁄₄oz/1¹⁄₂ tbsp butter

900g–1.2kg/2–2¹⁄₂lb fresh broad
* beans, shelled*

1 large parsley sprig

150ml/¹⁄₄ pint/²⁄₃ cup double or
* whipping cream*

3 egg yolks

a few drops of lemon juice

30ml/2 tbsp chopped fresh parsley

salt and freshly ground black pepper

M elt the butter in a saucepan and stir in the beans. Cook for 2–3 minutes, then add the parsley sprig, seasoning and enough water just to cover the beans. Cover the pan tightly, bring to boiling point and then immediately lower the heat and cook very gently for 15–20 minutes, shaking the pan occasionally, until the beans are tender and no liquid remains. Remove the pan from the heat, discard the parsley and leave to cool slightly.

Mix the cream with the egg yolks and stir into the beans. Reheat gently, stirring all the time, until the sauce coats the back of the spoon: do not boil.

Add a few drops of lemon juice and adjust the seasoning. Sprinkle with the chopped parsley and serve.

COOK'S TIP

If the beans are not as fresh as you would like and if you have the time and patience, slip off the outer skin of each bean. The bright green inner bean is wonderfully sweet and tender.

BAKED MARROW IN PARSLEY SAUCE

This creamy parsley sauce is a really glorious way of enriching a simple and modest vegetable.

Serves 4

1 small young marrow, about
  900g/2lb
30ml/2 tbsp olive oil
15g/¹/₂oz/1 tbsp butter
1 onion, chopped
15ml/1 tbsp plain flour
300ml/¹/₂ pint/1¹/₄ cups milk and
  single cream, mixed
30ml/2 tbsp chopped fresh parsley
salt and freshly ground black pepper

COOK'S TIP
*If liked, remove the lid for the
final 5 minutes of cooking to
gratinize the top of the dish.*

Preheat the oven to 180°C/350°F/Gas 4 and cut the marrow into rectangular pieces, about 5 x 2.5cm/2 x 1in. Heat the oil and butter in a flameproof casserole and fry the onion over a gentle heat until very soft. Add the marrow and sauté for 1–2 minutes, then stir in the flour. Cook for a few minutes and stir in the milk and cream mixture.

Add the parsley and seasoning and stir well to mix. Cover and cook in the oven for 30–35 minutes. Serve hot.

FENNEL TABBOULEH WITH PARSLEY

Tabbouleh is famous for using huge quantities of fresh parsley. Here fennel adds a lovely aniseed flavour, while the pomegranate gives a tantalizing sweetness.

Serves 6

225g/8oz/1 cup bulgur wheat

1 pomegranate

2 fennel bulbs

1 small fresh red chilli, seeded and
    finely chopped

1 celery stick, finely sliced

30ml/2 tbsp olive oil

finely grated rind and juice
    of 2 lemons

6–8 spring onions, chopped

90ml/6 tbsp chopped fresh mint

90ml/6 tbsp chopped fresh parsley

salt and freshly ground black pepper

Soak the bulgur wheat in enough cold water to cover for 30 minutes. Drain through a sieve, pressing out any excess water using the back of a spoon. Scoop out the pomegranate seeds and place in a large bowl. Halve the fennel bulbs, cut into very fine slices and add to the pomegranate seeds with the chilli, celery, olive oil, lemon rind and juice, spring onions, mint and parsley. Add the bulgur wheat and seasoning and stir well. Cover and set aside for 30 minutes before serving.

PASTA RAPIDO WITH PARSLEY PESTO

Here's a fresh, lively sauce to perk up pasta. It's similar to traditional pesto but uses almonds instead of pine nuts and parsley instead of basil.

Serves 4

450g/1lb dried pasta
75g/3oz/³⁄4 cup whole almonds
50g/2oz/¹⁄2 cup flaked almonds,
    toasted
40g/1¹⁄2oz fresh flat leaf parsley
2 garlic cloves, crushed
45ml/3 tbsp olive oil
45ml/3 tbsp lemon juice
5ml/1 tsp sugar
25g/1oz/¹⁄3 cup Parmesan cheese,
    grated

COOK'S TIP
The other half of the sauce will keep in a screw-topped jar in the fridge for up to 10 days.

Cook the pasta in plenty of salted water according to the instructions on the packet. Toast the whole and flaked almonds separately under a moderate grill until golden brown.

Place the parsley in a food processor and finely chop. Add the whole almonds and process again until very finely chopped. Add the garlic, olive oil, lemon juice, sugar and 250ml/8fl oz/1 cup boiling water. Blend to a smooth sauce. Drain the pasta and combine with half of the sauce. Top with Parmesan cheese and toasted flaked almonds.

GNOCCHI WITH PARSLEY SAUCE

A mushroom and parsley sauce brings an exquisite flavour to these Italian potato dumplings.

Serves 4

450g/1lb peeled floury potatoes
450g/1lb peeled pumpkin, chopped
2 egg yolks
about 200g/7oz/1¾ cups plain flour
pinch of ground allspice
1.5ml/¼ tsp ground cinnamon
pinch of grated nutmeg
finely grated rind of ½ orange
50g/2oz/⅔ cup Parmesan cheese,
    shaved
salt and freshly ground black pepper

For the sauce

30ml/2 tbsp olive oil
1 shallot
175g/6oz fresh chanterelles or oyster
    mushrooms, sliced
10ml/2 tsp butter
150ml/¼ pint/⅔ cup crème fraîche
a little milk or water
75ml/5 tbsp chopped fresh parsley

Cook the potatoes in simmering salted water for about 20 minutes until tender. Drain and set aside. Place the pumpkin in a bowl, cover and microwave on full power for 8 minutes. Alternatively, wrap the pumpkin in foil and bake at 180°C/350°F/Gas 4 for 30 minutes. Drain well, add to the potatoes and then pass through a vegetable mill into a bowl. Add the egg yolks, flour, spices, orange rind and seasoning and mix to make a soft dough, adding more flour if the mixture is too soft.

Bring a large pan of salted water to the boil and dredge a work surface with plain flour. Spoon the gnocchi mixture into a piping bag fitted with a 1cm/½in plain nozzle. Pipe on to the floured surface to make a 15cm/6in sausage. Roll in flour and cut into 2.5cm/1in pieces. Repeat the process, making more sausage shapes. Mark each lightly with a fork and cook for 3–4 minutes in the boiling water. If cooking in batches, keep the gnocchi warm in a covered dish while cooking the remainder.

Make the sauce. Heat the oil in a non-stick frying pan and fry the shallot until softened but not browned. Add the mushrooms, cook briefly and then add the butter. Stir to melt and stir in the crème fraîche. Simmer briefly and adjust the consistency with milk or water. Add the parsley and season to taste with salt and pepper.

Lift the gnocchi out of the water with a slotted spoon and place in warmed soup bowls. Spoon the sauce over the top and scatter with Parmesan cheese shavings.